Wood Joinery for Beginners Handbook

The Essential Joinery Guide with Tools, Techniques, Tips and Starter Projects

Stephen Fleming

Bonus Booklet

Thanks for purchasing the book. In addition to the content, we are also providing an additional booklet consisting of Monthly planner and Project Schedule template for your first project.

It contains valuable information about woodworking and leathercraft.

Download the booklet by typing the below link.

http://bit.ly/leatherbonus

Cheers!

Table of Contents

1. Preface

This is the fifth book in my DIY series after the ***Woodworking for Beginners Handbook.*** This book takes the discussion about woodworking a step further with a focus on various types of joinery and their applications.

When I first started woodcraft, I was desperately looking for a go-to guide about the processes and tools I would need.

The content I found online was total information overload and wasn't even presented sequentially. The books I looked at were either focused on just a few processes or assumed that I already had the necessary information. A lot of the books were also very dated.

There are two ways of learning; one is learning from SMEs (Subject Matter Experts) with years of experience, and the other is people who are just a few steps ahead of you in their journey.

I fall into the latter group. I'm five years into this hobby and still learning from the experts.

I still remember the initial doubts I had and the tips that helped me.

This book is for those who are still running their first lap (0-3 years) in wood crafting and want to have a holistic idea of the processes and tools they will need for joinery. The book also discusses Japanese and CNC joinery.

I have included photographs of realistic beginner projects, and I will explain the process and standard operating procedures associated with them.

In the last chapter, Appendix, I have provided a glossary of joinery terms.

Cheers, and let's start the journey

Stephen Fleming

2. Basics of Joinery

What is Joinery? A Definition

Joinery is a fundamental part of woodworking that can be found practically everywhere in the making of furniture, windows, doors, and floor coverings.

Although the vital function of joinery is to **hold wood together** firmly, it can additionally be used to make the wood piece more attractive.

Joinery can either involve a simple process of wood being toenailed or glued together or, it can entail a far more complex joining of two pieces of wood.

The team evaluating joinery technique

Here are a few definitions to make things more clear:

- *Joinery is a part of woodworking that involves **joining together pieces of wood or lumber**, to produce more complex woods.*
- *Some wood joints **employ fasteners, bindings, or adhesives**, while others use only wood elements.*
- *The characteristics of wooden joints - **strength, flexibility, toughness, appearance**, etc. - derive from the properties of the materials involved and the purpose of the joint.*
- *Therefore, different joinery techniques are used to meet differing requirements.*

Refer: (https://en.wikipedia.org/wiki/Woodworking_joints)

Carpentry vs. Joinery

Many people are uncertain about the difference between a joiner and a carpenter. If you need a task to be completed, that involves wood, who do you call?

Both carpenters and joiners share numerous qualities; nevertheless, they are described differently, depending on your area - the south of England tends to use the term 'carpenter,' while the north of England tends to say 'joiner.' Both a carpenter and a joiner are tradesmen within the building and construction sector, and both primarily work with wood.

Joiners

A joiner is an artisan who makes or **joins the wood**, generally **in a workshop**, whereas a carpenter constructs wooden pieces **on-site**. In straightforward terms, a joiner makes the timber that a carpenter then fixes on-site. A joiner, therefore, is generally connected to making doors, windows, staircases, and equipped furnishings that are usually made in a workshop off-site because heavy machinery is needed.

Carpenters

A carpenter is typically an expert in more prominent aspects, such as building sand fitting roofing trusses, stud work, and floors on-site by cutting as well as fitting pieces together, making use of a range of materials and devices. Carpenters are accountable for **setting up and building a structure**.

Bespoke Joinery

Bespoke relates to creating something based on someone's unique specifications. Store-bought furniture such as closets, shelving systems, TV systems, and even closets can't be personalized and so won't be tailored to the nuances of a room. Custom joinery also adds value to your home.

Brief Introduction to the Joinery Process

Joinery entails attaching wood pieces of timber. Types of joints involve:

Fasteners
- Screws (open, plugged, capped).
- Pocket screws.
- Nails (hammer and also pneumatic).

Bindings
- Metal straps, metal corners, corners.
- Material straps: fabric, natural leather.

Adhesive
- Wood adhesive: Glue creates a more robust attachment.
- Water swelling.

Wood aspects

- Dowel: A wooden rod set right into both blocks of adjoining wood.
- Biscuit: A small wooden biscuit formed piece is set into both pieces of adjoining wood.
- Spline: Comparable to the biscuit, however, the "spline" runs the joint's whole size.
- Corner blocks: Square or triangular blocks positioned at a joint to attach both blocks of wood.

Commonly used joints in woodworking:

Butt joint: A piece of timber is joined to another part of the wood. This is the simplest, as well as the weakest joint.

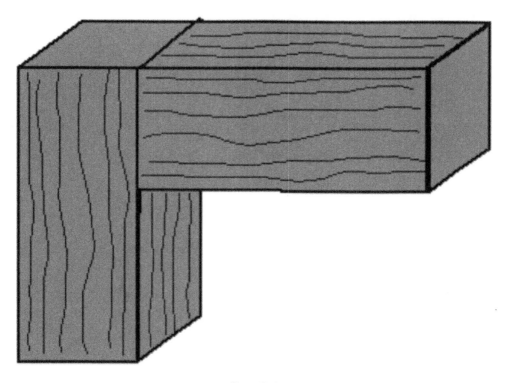

Butt Joint
(Photo Reference: Jomegat at the English Wikipedia / CC BY-SAhttp://creativecommons.org/licenses/by-sa/3.0/)

Miter joint: Comparable to a butt joint, the only difference being both pieces have been placed at a 45-degree angle.

Miter Joint

Lap joints: One wood of wood will overlap the other, as shown below.

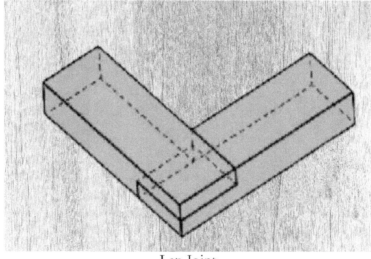

Lap Joint

Box joint: Also called a finger joint, this is used for the edges of boxes. It includes several lap joints at the ends of two boards.

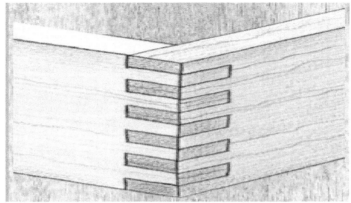

Box or Finger Joint

Dovetail joint: A kind of box joint where the fingers are secured via diagonal cuts.

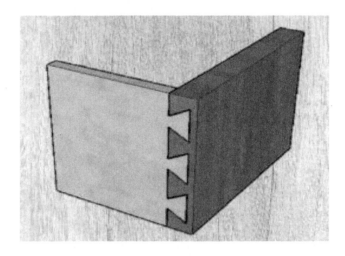

Dovetail Joint

Dado joint: A port is cut across the grain in one piece for another piece to slip into it. Shelves in a bookcase have ports cut into the sides, for instance.

Dado Joint

Groove joint: The port is cut with the grain. After that, one piece is fixed with the other along the grooves.

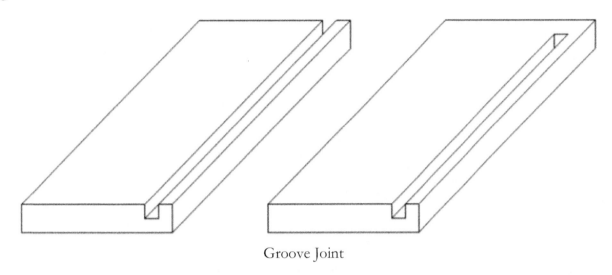

Groove Joint

Tongue and also groove. Each wood has a groove cut entirely along one side, and a narrow, deep ridge (the tongue) is on the opposite side. If the tongue is unattached, it is a spline joint.

Mortise and Tenon

Mortise, as well as tenon: A stub (the tenon) will fit snugly into a hole cut out for it (the mortise). This is a feature of Mission Style furniture and is also the traditional approach to the jointing framework and panel participants in doors, windows, and closets.

Wood Squaring

For wood to be correctly joined, crucial actions have to be taken to guarantee optimal strength as well as integrity, appropriate symmetry, and visual aesthetics. One of these is done by **squaring the wood**.

Natural wood defects

Wane: This is the visibility of bark or the absence of wood fiber along the edges of a wood piece. It doesn't impact the strength of the wood. Nonetheless, it is restricted in framing lumber because of the loss of a nailing side.

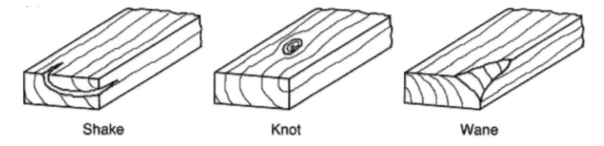

| Shake | Knot | Wane |

Shake: It is a longitudinally split in the wood, which occurs between or through the yearly growth rings. Shake often happens because of the tree shaking in the wind.

Knot: One of the most noticeable grading attributes is a knot, which is an imperfection in the wood. Knots affect the strength of wood.

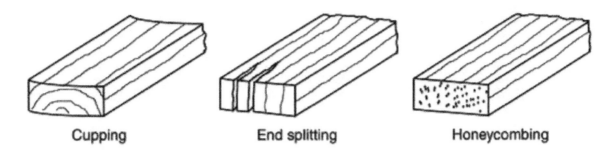

Seasonal Defects

Hole: If a knot develops through the piece of lumber, it creates an opening. Openings can likewise be created by natural creatures or during the manufacturing process. The opening can either extend totally through the timber or just partly, which is then usually described as a surface pit. A hole and a knot of the same size will affect the wood in the same way.

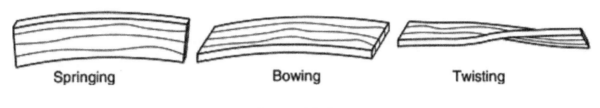

Seasonal Defects

Squaring the timber:

The term "square" describes a perfect 90 ° angle. To put it simply, every face of the lumber is 90 ° to the surrounding side. When wood is aligned, if it is square, the two kinds of wood will create ideal angles to one another.

No light should be visible between boards. This assures that the adhesive is appropriately sealed without any gaps.

Squaring timber starts with the jointer. Plane the faces initially, then the side. As soon as one side is planed, use the table saw to square the last edge. As soon as the sides of the two woods of lumber are squared, you can begin gluing.

Lining up the grain:

When gluing two blocks of wood together along the side, use alternate end grain patterns. This protects against the constructed wood cupping.

3. Tools of Joinery

Fasteners

A metal fastener is a type of tool, such as a nail or screw, which joins or affixes two or more woods together. The most common steel fasteners used in woodworking joinery are:

1. Nails (hammer and also pneumatic).

2. Timber Screws (open, connected, topped, putty).

3. Bolts.

4. Pocket screws.

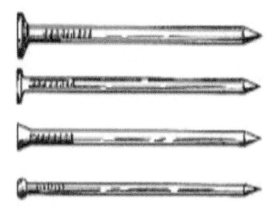

Type of Nails: Top to Bottom: Usual/General, Box, Casing, Finishing

Nails:
There are many types of nails you will use in woodworking: Two of them are:

- Usual/General Nails
- Finishing Nails

General nails have a flat head and used in construction projects.

Finishing nails have a little head and are designed for "punching" or penetrating the wood with a device called a hole strike. By doing so, the nail is pressed right into the timber, and putty is applied over it. This "filler" hides the nail from view and also helps to preserve the all-natural color of the timber.

Wood Screws:

Unlike the smooth shanks of many nails, screw fastenings have a threaded shank with machined spirals shaped in away that the screw might be inserted or removed by turning the head.

There are two typical thread types, coarse threaded as well as fine threaded. Coarse threaded spirals are further apart as well as much deeper than fine threaded spirals and ought to be used in softwoods.

As hardwood grain is a lot more compressed, fine threaded screws should be used.

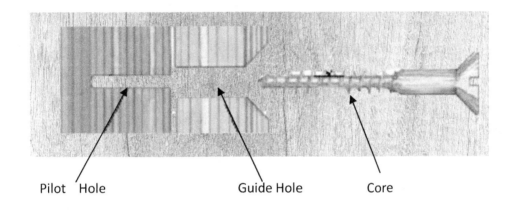

Pilot Hole   Guide Hole   Core

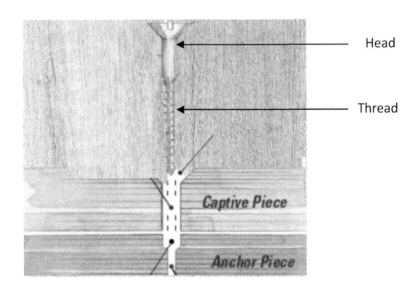

Head

Thread

Captive Piece

Anchor Piece

Bolts:

Bolts aren't like screws or nails as they are not driven into the timber. Instead, the hole as per the dimension of the bolt must be pierced in both wood pieces to be joined

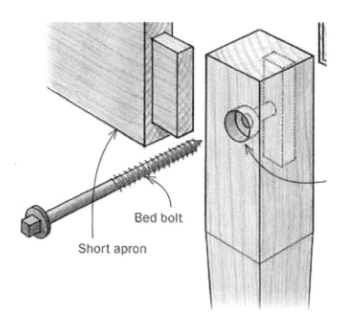

Bed bolt

Short apron

Pocket Screws:

Pocket screws get their name from the fact that they are recessed into the timber in an angled countersink called a pocket. They offer fast, solid, and uniformly matched joinery.

There is little difference between a pocket screw and a basic timber screw, though the head is larger and not tapered, and the screw tip is made to self-tap.

Pocket openings are built using a jig - a device used to hold wood.

Pocket Screws

Splines and Rods

Wooden rods or splines might also be placed, glued, and afterward secured together to provide toughness to wood joints.

Standard rods, as well as spline joints, are:

- **Doweled joints:** A wood rod, called a dowel, is placed and glued in both blocks of wood and then clamp. In the old days, water was used rather than glue. This is because water causes timber to swell, so the dowel would certainly swell in the timber as well as safeguard it.

- **Biscuit joints:** After cutting a slot right into the two blocks of wood to be joined, an oval-shaped, highly-dried, and pressed wood biscuit (generally constructed from beech wood) is

17

covered with adhesive and also put in place. The boards are then clamped together until the attachment is full.

- **Spline joints:** A spline is a thin piece of timber inserted right into two matching ports cut into timber joints, much like a biscuit. A spline is typically added to beautify the job.

Glue and Clamps

Clamping and gluing is the process for attaching wood with the force and adhesion necessary to ensure strong timber joints.

This is completed by utilizing clamps and wood glue. Remarkably, when the wood is glued together, it develops a stronger-than-wood bond.

This fact alone makes gluing a valid alternative to consider when sticking timber together.

Various other techniques might be used to help in the process, such as biscuits, dowels, nails, and screws, but an adequately glued butt joint is not to be underestimated.

The Gluing Method:

Before gluing, make sure you have all the necessary devices and tools on the table with you.

First, decide what type of clamp you will use. A clamp is a tool used for holding two pieces of wood together.

There are many different types of clamps, and all of these vary in the level of pressure they can apply.

Different Clamps

Below are the most popular wood clamps:

- Bar clamp
- Timber clamp or hand screw clamp
- C-clamp
- Spring clamp
- Screw clamp
- Strap or band
- Screw clamp
- Toggle clamp
- Pipeline clamp
- One-handed bar clamp
- Miter clamp

The type of clamp you select will be based on the dimension and the amount of pressure you require. Pipeline clamps, for example, are long and have the greatest cranking power. On the other hand, spring clamps are small and have less compression strength.

As soon as you have identified the clamp for your task, you just need to go out and get it. A clamping device is any type of gadget helpful for the gluing procedure.

Below are some clamping tools:

- **Cauls:** Stiff wood planks that are clamped to panel glue-ups, on top of each other, to maintain the specific boards' alignment.

- **Wax paper**: Prevents wooden woods from sticking to the table.

- **Squares**: Allow you to see if the wood is square (90 °).

- **Wet paper towel:** Excess glue is the enemy!

4. Types of Joinery- Detailed Discussion

1. Butt Joint-Basic

Butt joints are one of the most basic approaches for connecting two pieces of timber. Also, while it isn't the toughest of joints, it is useful in some situations.

You can find out exactly how to make a butt joint by utilizing the correct strategy to guarantee that your butt joints are as strong as possible.

As shown in the picture, a butt joint is where one piece of wood is butted against another and joined with adhesive.

Screws or nails typically enhance the joint.

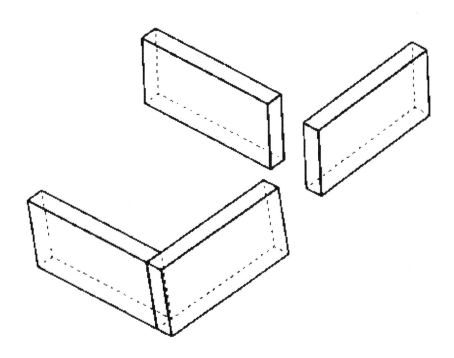

Basic Butt Joint

Square Cuts Are Key:

The trick to a top-quality butt joint is to ensure that the two boards are cut as square as possible. This is best done with a miter saw, although top-quality results can be obtained utilizing a circular saw and a design square, provided that the angle of the blade of the round saw is set to zero degrees.

Types of Butt Joint

Glue Offers Strength:

The strength of a butt joint comes from the glue in the joint.

However, there are two issues with using glue as the only method of holding the connection together.

Initially, when the glue is applied to the end grain of a board, it tends to saturate right into the wood far more than glue on the side of the grain. The end grain is the most porous part of the wood, so you might need to apply a little bit more adhesive.

If utilizing hardwood for your task, make sure to pre-drill the pilot holes before placing screws into the joint.

General Strength of the Butt Joint

The strength of the joint depends on the straightness of the side (not necessarily the squareness) and the positioning of the timber fibers.

This joint doesn't require any type of machine used on its parts. The only preparation required is the planing or jointing of the sides for straightness.

With modern adhesives, this joint can be as strong as the timber itself.

One benefit of the butt joint is speed. Nevertheless, without a way to join the two edges for a level joint, you're limited to putting together pieces no longer than 48 inches.

Ways to make butt joint stronger

- Use support from iron; edge pieces are readily available in any equipment shop.

- T plates are excellent if your pieces are out of sight.

T-Plate   Plywood Gusset

- The plywood gusset is likewise an excellent strengthener for butt joints.

- This joinery strengthener is especially useful if you make boxes and cabinets.

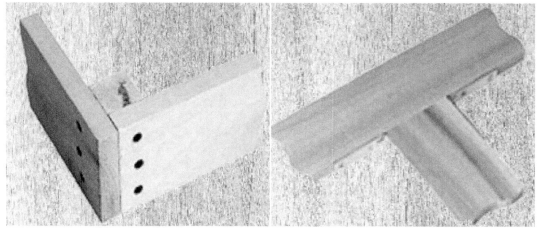

| Wooden Block | Corner Brace |

- A woodblock is commonly used to make table structures stronger.

- It is a straightforward method to make your edges with butted joints sufficiently solid to sustain table legs.

2. Mitered Butt Joint

A butt joint is basic and involves wood pieces that are joined at 90 degrees. It isn't one of the prettiest of joints, though, as completion grain of one of the two boards will be visible.

Mitered Joint

When you want something that looks nicer, try a mitered butt joint.

It will not be any more durable than a conventional butt joint, but you will also not see the end grain.

Angles need to be specific:

Like with a fundamental butt joint, the most crucial element of producing a mitered butt joint is to cut the angles correctly. For this, you'll need a compound miter saw.

The first step is to figure out the joint's final angle and divide it by two. For a square link (90-degrees), you'll need to make a 45-degree angle cut on both boards to allow joining.

If the two pieces are the same width, the two edges should join flawlessly.

This joint could be used while building various other joints of other angles. As an example, if you were making an octagonal-shaped image framework, each of the eight edges would be 45-degrees (instead of the 90degrees in the previous instance). Thus, you would cut 22 1/2- degree angles on each end to create the butt joints.

Glue holds the joint:

Just like with an essential butt joint, adhesive holds the joint together.

Nonetheless, both sides of the adhesive joint will be on permeable end grain. You will likely need to use even more woodworking glue than when gluing on side grain.

TIP: Dry-fit your pieces before using adhesive to be sure of the final fit. For example, if you're making a picture frame, cut all lengths and angles, then cross-check the structure so that there is no gap between the wood pieces.

Example of furniture using Mitered Joint

Use mechanical bolts for strength:

Similar to a standard butt joint, there isn't a great deal of strength in a mitered butt joint.

So, you might want to reinforce the joint using nails, brads, or screws to provide lateral strength to the joint.

If using hardwood, pre-drill before mounting screws to avoid splitting.

3. Spline Joint

A spline joint is created when a wood spline is placed and glued into the slot or groove of another woodworking joint, usually a butt, side, or mitered joint.

The spline serves to reinforce the joint and keep both areas aligned. This small enhancement adds substantial strength to whatever joint it's used on.

The spline is made from plywood, hardwood, or the exact same material as the joint being strengthened. For the ultimate in toughness, the natural wood grain needs to be oriented to make sure that it's aligned up with the joint on the work surface.

Splines should never ever be pushed into the grooves, which can cause them to misshape or divide. Rather, they must slide in quickly, however, with no side play, to enable adequate space for the glue to create a solid joint.

Miter spline

The miter spline is excellent for strengthening picture frameworks, mirror frames, and cabinet face frames that utilize mitered corners. Tiny appealing boxes can use contrasting tinted splines with mitered edges for visual effect, in addition to strengthening the joints.

The splines are typically no greater than a third of the total thickness of the workpieces. It's ideal for cutting the spline oversize and then trimming and sanding smooth once the adhesive has dried. A dry-fit before glue-up is recommended.

Spline between Miter and at corner slot

Miter spline joints look fantastic when utilizing contrasting colors. A light tinted spline set in a darker wood will certainly attract the eye and also highlight the joint.

Side spline

Edge splines are typically used to make larger panels out of several narrower boards.

The most common side spline joint has the groove and spline running along the wood piece.

If the look isn't that important, plywood makes an outstanding spline. If appearance is your main concern, the spline can be made from solid timber of your choice.

The stopped edge spline is similar to a quit dado joint because the groove is cut short of the completion of the board, although on both ends in this situation.

It is generally used for the tops of hardwood tables as well as various other types of furniture for which the craftsman would like the additional strength.

A simple plywood spline can be used without impacting the appearance of the joint.

As we know, the groove can be cut with a table saw, this is possibly much easier than using a router table with a slotting bit.

The utility of Spline Joint

The purpose is to reinforce as well as straighten the edges. A spline can be used as a substitute for the tongue and groove.

- Splines for toughness: Splines are commonly used to strengthen miter and butt joints

- Splines as accents: Dress up a joint using contrasting timbers

- The framework of the joint: Use the right proportions to ensure toughness and security

4. Half-Lap Joint

These are among the most basic of woodworking joints. There are times where they are the best option for joining two wood pieces together.

A half-lap joint is where two blocks of wood, of the same density, have half of the wood removed to ensure that no thickness is added at the joint.

These joints function well for right-angle links. Both boards have material removed so that they join seamlessly.

When to utilize half-lap joints:

Half-lap joints function well when using one to a two-inch thick wood, such as in dressers & work desks, especially where drawers will be set up.

The half-lap includes strength to the interior and a framework without adding additional height. The half-lap joint can be reasonably strong when used properly.

Nonetheless, be advised that thin pieces of wood might deteriorate in strength after cutting half of the lap to make this joint. So, use this joint when the wood is thick to preserve the stability of the board after half of the wood is removed.

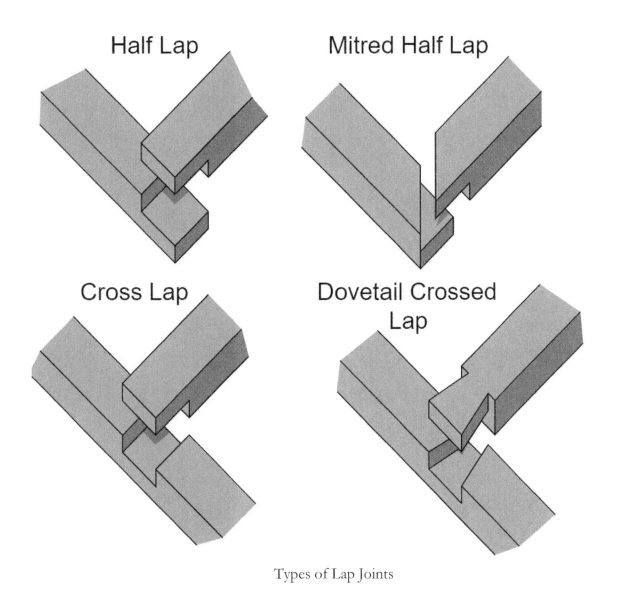

Types of Lap Joints

How to cut half-lap joints:

Many devices can be used to cut half-laps. However, my favorite is a piled dado set on a radial arm saw.

You'll need a couple of pieces of scrap wood to get the set perfect, but once you have the appropriate elevation setting on the radial arm, you'll be making plenty of half-lap joints in a short time.

In the absence of a radial arm saw, you can achieve the same with a dado set on a table saw.

Make sure to utilize your miter scale to guide the wood through the blade.

Never use the fence on the table saw for crosscuts, as the fence can make the wood bind.

When you have a cut every quarter inch between the edges of the joint, use a hammer to clean up the thin pieces.

After finishing up the joint with a chisel, you must have a wholly developed half-lap joint.

Putting together the joint:

When you're ready to set up the joint, put some woodworker's glue on both mating surfaces.

Put the other wood of wood in place and adjust both to their final placements. Then, join the wood pieces with a few wood screws.

The adhesive will be the strength of the joint, but the screws are needed to hold it together until the glue dries.

5. Tongue and Groove Joint

The tongue and groove joint is a joint attached edge to edge with two or more pieces of wood.

It is made with one side being composed of a slot that runs down the length of the wood and a tongue that fits into the slot.

Groove Tongue

This groove and tongue feature allows a stable and aesthetically pleasing joint that can be used in floorboards, lining boards, wood paneling, and tabletops.

This joint type is simple and enables a limited fit that has a lot of area for adhesives.

These joints can be tough to make without the right machinery. You are more likely to purchase wood with this joint already in it, such as lining boards.

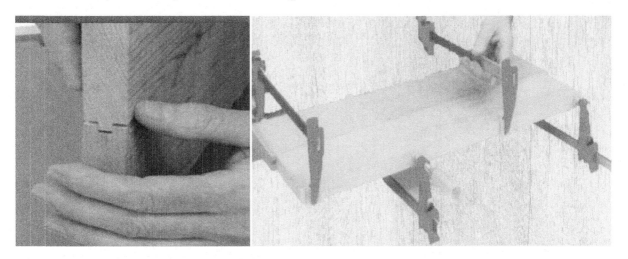

Check Fitment Glue and Clamp

Additionally, this is used more as a function in furniture, so it doesn't typically require a lot of timber.

Step 1: This joint is only used in timber boards. Therefore, the first thing to do is to gauge and cut up some boards of the appropriate length.

Step 2: This step is not entirely essential if you have some experience using a router, but otherwise, you need to note the wood and to get ends on your boards.

Step 3: This action requires a router bench to produce an effective joint, and the first thing you should do is begin with a router bit to reduce the groove. After the groove has actually been made, use an extra router bit to cut the tongue.

Step 4: See if the joint fits tightly, and if it does, you can add adhesive and clamp the boards together, which will interlace your tongue and groove joints.

Tip: The lining boards already have a tongue and groove joints, which makes this option much easier for individuals with time restraints or unskilled woodworkers.

Gluing: The suggested adhesive for drifting installment is tongue and groove engineered floor covering adhesive. Glue placement is critical. The adhesive needs to be positioned along the groove's topside, the complete size of the grooved side, and the end.

An additional **advantage** of this joint is the adhesive surface availability. The single **disadvantage** might be that the joint is visible from the end of the panel. The tongue-and-groove joint is usually used to make wider panels from narrower boards, such as when constructing **tabletops, doors,** or **architectural paneling.**

6. Mortise and Tenon Joint

The mortise and tenon joints have been used for centuries by woodworkers due to their combination of superior toughness and simplicity.

They are usually used when one wood of wood is joined with various others at 90-degree angles but may be used at a somewhat lower angle in certain conditions. Remember that the joint is toughest when the two blocks of wood are at right angles to each other.

Mortise

Tenon

The key behind a mortise and tenon joint is that a piece of wood is inserted right into the other and held in place with a fastener.

Today, a lot of woodworkers use adhesive to safeguard the tenon inside the mortise, but in years passed, woodworkers would style the tenons to make sure that a wedge or dowel protects them.

Making Tenon:

A rectangle pin cut from the end of the wood is tenon.

While tenons can be cut by hand, contemporary woodworkers will typically use a band saw, or a tenoning jig on a table.

When cutting a tenon, beware not to remove excess material, as thinner tenons lead to weak joints.

Cutting the Mortise:

Generally, mortises were cut into the receiving piece of wood using a chisel. Today, several woodworkers use a mortise, which uses a little drill bit encased in a four-sided sculpt.

Several drill press suppliers offer optional mortising attachments, making the drill press a far more functional machine.

To cut a mortise, note where to cut, and after that sink the bit right into the material, taking little bites at a time.

Establish the depth enough to include the entire length of thereon, make it no deeper than absolutely needed (unless you are developing a through-tenon). When completed, use a sharp chisel to clean up any remaining rough spots.

Joint Fitting:

When the mortise and tenon have both been completed, dry-fit the tenon into the mortise.

The fit has to be snug, but not too limiting. As soon as all joints have been formed and its time for setting up, use glue on both the tenon and inside the mortise. Cover all surface areas equally using a tiny brush.

A good rule of thumb when developing mortise, as well as tenon joints, is to cut the mortise first. Keep the tenon bit wider for the dry test of the joint.

Double Mortise Tenon Joint

When this joint is used:

Mortise &tenon is typically used when corner joints require tough frameworks for making things such as doors, tables, home windows, and beds.

A rectangular slot is described as a mortise cut, and it is cut into the (specific) center of the end piece of timber to ensure that it will take in the protrusion fitting (the tenon), thus making a clean, solid joint.

After it has been glued and well equipped, the wood joints will not ove and will be really tough to pull apart.

To ensure that the mortise is one-third as thick as the timber, it has to have precise measurements.This is to avoid any kind of splitting of the mortise and tenon breakage.

7. BiscuitJoint

In comparison to joints such as edge-to-edge joints, miter joints, T-joints, and edge joints, the most effective is biscuit joints.

Properly-cut biscuit joints are reliable as well as precise, particularly when cutting slots with a woodworking device called a biscuit joiner (or plate joiner).

What is a biscuit?
A thin, oval-shaped wood piece, typically made from beech wood, is called a biscuit.

When glued into slots precisely cut by the biscuit cutter, the dampness from the adhesive causes the biscuit to swell and tighten up the joint.

Tools Required for making Biscuit Joint

- A plate jointer, also known as a biscuit jointer.
- A saw.
- Measuring tape.
- Square.
- Wood glue/ Woodworker's adhesive.
- Clamps.
- Lumber.

Different sizes of Biscuits

Biscuits are commonly found in three sizes:

- 0 - 5/8" x 1-3/4"
- 10 - 3/4" x 2-1/8"
- 20 - 1" x 2-3/8"

Biscuit cutters must have the capability to cut all three sizes precisely.

What Size Biscuit to Utilize?

As a basic guideline, using the biggest biscuit will offer the highest amount of toughness to the joint.

Most of the time, use # 20 biscuits. However, when working on narrower material, use a button to smaller biscuits.

Edge-to-Edge Joints:

One of the most typical biscuit joints is edge-to-edge joints. This is typically used for gluing tabletops of varying sizes of the same thickness, where biscuits are used along the long sides of the boards.

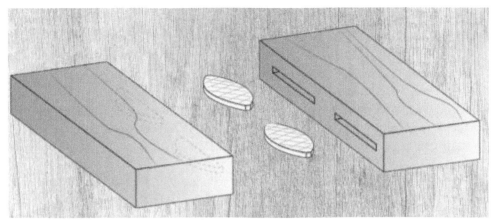

Edge-to-Edge Joints

To glue a tabletop of different boards, lay the boards side-by-side with each board's end grain turned opposite to the previous board. This will keep the tabletop stable if the boards expand or contract.

Once the boards are in the correct positions, use a pencil to make marks across the joints every 4-6". These will be the centerlines for the biscuit ports.

Next, adjust your biscuit joiner depending on the size of a biscuit. In the case of edge-to-edge joints, you'll most likely use the large # 20 dimension.

Place the overview fence on top of the wood (perpendicular to the edge) and straighten the cutting guide with the pencil mark.

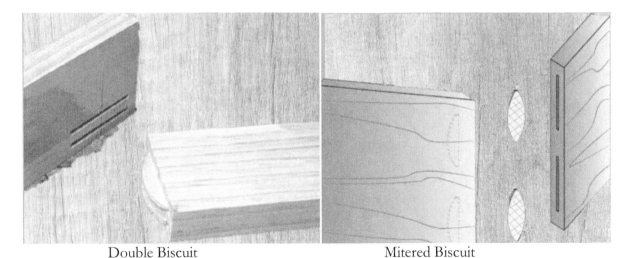

Double Biscuit   Mitered Biscuit

Hold the fence in place, start the saw, and when the electric motor gets to full speed, push the blade into the wood until it doesn't go any further.

After that, withdraw the blade totally and repeat for the following mark.

When all of the ports are ready, apply glue evenly throughout the slots, edge, and place the biscuits.

You'll want to quickly glue each edge of the tabletop and afterward secure the entire piece. Use the clamps to make sure that the entire voids are completely closed. However, be careful to avoid squeezing so hard that the adhesive leaks out.

If any glue does squeeze out of the joints, make sure to wipe it off right away to avoid affecting the surface later on.

8. Pocket Joints

Pocket joints are like a screw that is driven diagonally through one board into another.

Pocket joints are similar to dowel joints and mortise & tenon joints.

For a pocket joint, the course for the screw should be pre-drilled to avoid splitting the head wood. While this can be done in other ways, a much more straightforward approach is using a pocket-hole jig. The screw is driven through the headboard right into the tailwood.

No glue is required, as the screw will hold the joint firmly, but the glue will add more strength to the joint.

Pocket Joint

Pocket Hole Jigs

Pocket Opening/Hole Jigs:

Improvements in pocket opening jig technology over the last few years have made it easier and more popular.

There are numerous styles of pocket joints, but the major one is a jig with a machined aluminum overview cylinder placed at a specific inclination.

After that, the jig is clamped to the headboard.

A bit that is the same size as the hole and is used to pierce the lightweight aluminum cylinder right into the headboard.

As soon as the pocket opening has been pierced into the headboard, the tailboard is clamped right into the area, and a screw is driven through the pocket opening directly into the tailboard.

If the glue is to be included in strengthening the joint, it needs to be placed on the mating surface area between the tailboard as well as the headboard before putting the screw(s).

Uses of Pocket Joints:

The most popular use for pocket joints is in face frameworks. There are many other possible applications, though. Pocket joints can be used to join sides to make a table or closet top.

They are likewise very efficient in affixing relatively thick edge banding to plywood or a tabletop.

Pocket joints can also be used to attach angled joints in woodworking jobs such as braces for leg rails.

Edge Joint   Example of Pocket Joints

Strength:

Pocket joints are stronger than mortise and tenon joints.

Use

- The pocket joint is mostly used in cabinet frames, face frames, and carcasses.
- Pocket hole joinery makes edging up limited versus tabletops and countertops - and keeps it there.
- Pocket hole joinery provides you with remarkably limited mitered photo framework joints without tough corner-clamping.
- Add extension jamb to a home window or door without visible fasteners. Pocket hole joints keep jambs in place as well as provide a limited, weather-sealed joint.
- Curves - Pocket opening joinery makes it simple to construct odd-angled components and also offers curved forms.

Jamb: A pre-hung door consists of a door hung on hinges and assembled in a **wood frame.

9. Dado Joint

Using a dado is practical and a reliable technique for linking two pieces of wood. When you learn how to cut a dado, you'll choose these woodworking joints that are specifically practical when constructing shelves or cabinet boxes.

This joint is a groove cut into one piece of timber right into which another piece of timber will fit snugly.

For example, when constructing a shelf using 3/4" thick wood, one would cut a 3/4" large groove right into the rack requirement and glue the rack in the slot.

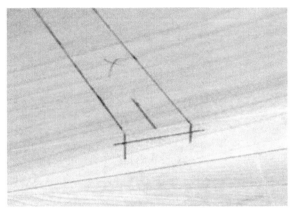
Marking before cutting Dado Joint

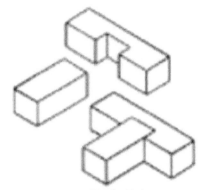
Dado Joint

Techniques for Cutting Dadoes:

There are a couple of techniques for cutting a dado. One of them is to make use of a table saw-based piled dado head cutter.

Broader dadoes can be cut with more than one round through the saw.

A piled dado head cutter collection only needs to be used on a table saw or some radial arm saws.

Do not attempt to make use of a stacked dado head cutting set on a round saw, as this would be exceptionally harmful.

One more option is a "totter" dado set. This is a solitary saw blade set on a flexible spindle. Changing the blade angle on the spindle will change the size of the dado.

While these are much cheaper than a piled dado head cutter set, the results are less reliable.

I would certainly resist the urge to purchase a wobble dado and save my money for a high-quality stacked dado collection.

I'm also concerned about safety while using a wobble blade.

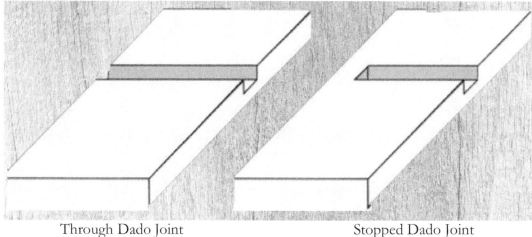

Through Dado Joint   Stopped Dado Joint

Cutting Dadoes with a Router:

Another well-known method for cutting dadoes is to use a straight cutting bit on a router.

When using a router to cut a dado, remember that you'll need to lower the speed quite a bit as well as readjust the deepness for more than one pass to keep from shedding the bit or timber. Use a straight edge to direct the router to guarantee a straight course.

Dado application in table

10. Rabbet Joint

A rabbet is like a dado that is cut into the side of the wood face, as opposed to in the center.

A rabbet is suitable for when a rack needs to be positioned back on a cabinet.

How to Cut a Rabbet:

Like a dado, one of the most common ways to cut a rabbet is with a stacked dado head cutting set on a table saw.

Commonly, a sacrificial strip of timber is positioned against the fencing, after which the sacrificial piece is placed against the dado collection.

This method will prevent damage to the table saw's fencing. Another common technique for cutting a rabbet is to use a router table with a straight cutting bit.

Use a feather board to hold the wood down to the table, which will ensure a regular cut.

The rabbet joint is much more powerful than a basic butt joint. It is also conveniently made either with two tables or radial-arm saw cuts (one into the face, the second right into the edge or end grain) or with one pass through a saw outfitted with a dado head.

The rabbet joint is used to establish backboards onto the rear of a case piece or to accommodate the glass on a mirror frame.

Basic Rabbet Joint

Dual Rabbet

The dual rabbet joint has a rabbet cut in both mating pieces. This joint is more durable than the basic rabbet for several reasons.

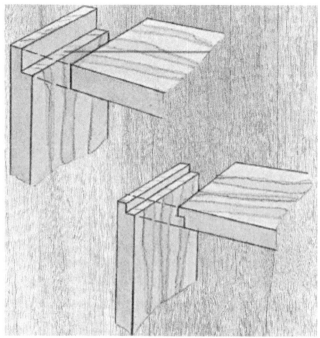

Rabbet and Dual Rabbet

The second rabbet supplies an extra gluing area to the joint as well as the additional ninety-degree shoulder.

Careful measurement, as well as cutting, is needed to make the joint fit without voids when cutting by hand.

They are made much more precisely on either a table saw or a router table.

This is an outstanding joint for the top corners of high bookcases as well as cupboards that won't be fitted with a face framework. The joint can be additionally boosted with equally spaced dowels driven in from the side.

Mitered Rabbet

The mitered rabbet might look challenging, yet with an excellent table saw or router table, it's not so bad. Once the equipment is appropriately set up, any kind of variety of these joints can be done quickly.

A mitered rabbet is probably one of the most attractive of all the variations of the rabbet joint.

It effectively hides completion grain and gives the joint a beautiful mitered appearance. You'll find this joint in luxury closets and cabinet boxes.

Mitered Rabbet

11. Dovetail Joints

a) Through Dovetail Joint

Dovetail is prized not only for its strength but also for its looks.

Dovetail joints can be tricky to style. However, dovetailing jigs and routers have made this joint much easier to perfect.

The dovetail joint is most commonly used in drawer building and construction.

However, there are several other kinds of joints that might be better suited to specific scenarios.

For instance, half-blind dovetails are used when the sides of the drawer need to connect straight with the face of the drawer.

Dovetails on cabinets should only be visible when the drawer is opened.

Blind dovetails are common in closet or box building and construction where the pins and tails must be wholly concealed.

Nevertheless, a section of the end grain of the tail wood will certainly be visible.

If the woodworker wants to hide the pins, tails as well as end grains, a mitered dovetail is the very best choice. Nonetheless, this is a complex joint, which takes a reasonable amount of time and patience to master.

There are numerous other variants on the classic dovetail, including rabbet through dovetails, mitered through dovetails, beveled dovetails, and box joints (which are essential dovetails with rectangle-shaped pins and tails).

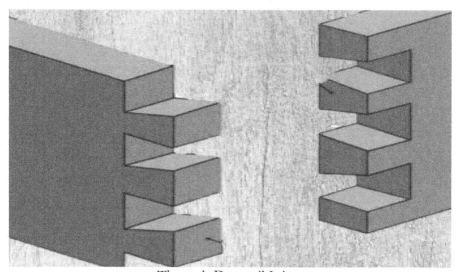

Through Dovetail Joint

Typical Creation of Through Dovetails:

Before the development of dovetailing jigs, dovetails were cut by hand, and some woodworkers today still choose this traditional technique.

The actions are fairly basic:

1. Plane the ends of the two pieces of wood in a wood square.

2. Mark the shoulder line of each piece, equal to the size of the adjacent piece.

3. Mark the ends of the tails at the desired angle.

4. Cut the tails with a dovetailing saw.

5. Remove the excess between the tails.

46

6. Utilizing the finished tails, note the pins on the contrary board.

7. Cut the pins and clean the waste.

Evaluate the joint's fit and cut more off the pins if required.

Utilizing a Dovetailing Jig:

To make a hole in dovetails with a dovetailing jig, the order is essentially the same. Mark the depth of the cut on the tailboard and insert it right into the jig.

Mount an appropriate dovetailing bit right into your router and cut the tails. Next, following the jig's directions, insert the pinboard into the jig in the proper location, switch to a straight cutting bit, and cut the pins.

Undoubtedly, the details for this procedure depend on the picked jig. Nonetheless, each dovetailing system includes a full, step-by-step set of instructions for cutting through dovetails.

Setting up:

Dovetails should fit snugly, but not be too tight. Consistently dry-fit your dovetails before you get to the last step, to guarantee your joint is perfect.

When dry-fitting through dovetails, they need to be a bit hard to take apart, but not so tough that you need a mallet to divide the parts.

When constructing through dovetails, spread a thin layer of woodworking glue on all surfaces of either the tails or the pins before placing the joint together.

Use a rubber club or a sacrificial block of timber with a claw hammer to stay clear of ruining the joint. Immediately wipe away any kind of extra glue.

The Secret to Perfect Dovetails:

If there is one rule to follow, no matter which technique you choose to cut your dovetails, it is this: *always cut the tails first, then cut the pins to fit the tails.*

It is much easier to take a bit more off the pins to make sure they fit the tails. Nonetheless, if you cut the pins first, the tails are far tougher to mark, increasing the probability of an incomplete dovetail joint.

b) Half-Blind Dovetail Joint

When connecting two pieces of wood, possibly the most prominent joint is the through dovetail.

The through dovetails are solid and look good. However, there are circumstances where it is not the right choice.

Like when connecting sides of a drawer directly to the drawer front, the ends of the tails will show in the drawer front if through dovetail is used.

In this case, the best sort of dovetail joint to use is the half-blind dovetail

Half Dovetail Joint

What is a Half-Blind Dovetail?

The half-blind dovetail is as precise as the name implies, i.e., only half of the joint is visible. This joint is almost as solid as the through dovetail but is used in scenarios such as the cabinet front situation outlined above.

Standard steps for cutting half-blind dovetails:

1. Plane the ends of both pieces of a wood square.

2. Mark the size of the tails, which is the size of the pinboard minus the lap. Make a shoulder line of the appropriate size around the tailboard.

3. Mark the tails at the preferred angle.

4. Cut the tails with a dovetailing saw.

5. Remove the waste between the tails using a bevel-edged chisel.

6. Using the finished tails, note the pins on the pinboard, lining up the shoulder cuts with the side of the pinboard opposite the lap.

7. Cut the pins and clean the waste using a chisel.

Joint only visible on the inside

Utilizing a Dovetailing Jig:

While almost all router-based dovetail jigs can puncture dovetails, only some specific methods can cut half-blind dovetails. Keep this in mind when buying a dovetail jig system for your store.

The treatment for cutting half-blind dovetails with a dovetail jig system is the same standard treatment. Mark the deepness of the cut on the tailboard based upon the size of the pinboard minus the lap.

Insert the tailboard right into the jig and cut the tails utilizing a suitable dovetailing router bit. Then, following the jig's guidelines, mark and cut the half-blind pins in the pinboard.

b) Sliding Dovetail Joint

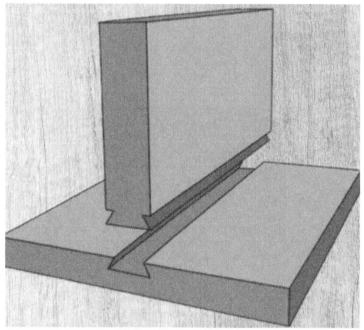

Sliding Dovetail Joint

Of all dovetail joints, the sliding dovetail might be the least well-known, particularly among woodworking beginners.

However, the sliding dovetail might be the most versatile of all dovetail joints.

It's not only handy for attaching two pieces of wood at a right-angle. It is also used to connect parts together in closet doors or cutting boards, for attaching table legs to stands and joining racks to cabinet instances.

This joint is made by cutting a single tail down the size of a board's side, which is slid right into a matching pin-shaped slot in the receiving item of wood. It is better to taper the slot in the receiving piece somewhat, to ensure that the joint is tighter towards the rear.

It will make the joint much more comfortable to slide in. It will also assist in maintaining the joint from splitting apart in the future.

Cutting a Sliding Dovetail Joint:

Typically, a sliding dovetail was made by cutting the tail and slotting it by hand and cleaning up the parts with a chisel.

Nevertheless, some modern-day dovetail jigs have the option to cut sliding dovetails with a router and a dovetail bit.

While this might remove some of the mystique of the joint, it makes the job a lot easier to do over and over, along with being a lot quicker.

If you have a dovetail jig that can cut a sliding dovetail joint, the actions for doing so need to be spelled out in the customer overview that comes with the dovetail jig.

12. Box Joint

The dovetail joint is a timeless, stunning & reliable method for attaching two pieces of wood. However, the dovetail joint can't be used in all cases.

For example, what if you need to attach two pieces of plywood?

Making use of dovetails to attach plywood would considerably boost the chances of peeling the plywood when examining the joint while dry fitting.

Box Joint

What happens if you do not have access to a dovetail jig and router?

This is if you don't want to go to the trouble of hand-sewing dovetails. Is there another alternative apart from dovetails to use in your woodworking tasks?

A simple alternative to the dovetail is the box joint.

As you can see, a box joint is similar to a dovetail, with the distinction of the rectangular fingers.

Naturally, you could always do it with a dovetail saw and a chisel. Choose a width for the fingers that will divide evenly right into the wood width.

If your wood is 6 inches wide, a half-inch finger will permit twelve fingers overall, six on each piece of wood.

The glued box joint has a high glued surface leading to a strong bond that is similar to a finger joint. Box joints are used for edges of boxes or box-like constructions, hence the name.

13. Bridle Joint

Bridle joints are similar to mortise and tenon joints.

The difference is in the dimension of the mortise and tenon. As these joints still have a mortise and tenon, they are durable and look appealing.

The distinction in the bridle joints and mortise and tenon stays in the size of the tenon and deepness of the mortise.

The tenon on this joint is as long as the deepness of the hardwood.

This allows both wood pieces to lock tightly. The new area allows the opportunity to add more glue, which makes it more robust.

These are popular joints for joining rails, legs, and stiles.

Bridle Joint Pros

- A less complicated option to the mortise and tenon joint
- Can shape joint set up without giving up on strength
- Great for creating slim frameworks
- One of the essential joints to cut
- Does not need mortising equipment

Bridle Joint Cons
- Can see the end grain

Types of Bridle Joint

Corner BridleJoints can be used as a more comfortable replacement for a haunched mortise and tenon joint, especially where the structure is to be skinned or covered (e.g., frames for loose, cushioned chair seats).

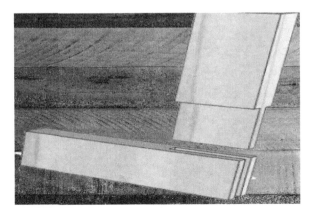

Corner Bridle

Tee Bridle Joints can be used as an easier option to a mortise as well as a tenon joint, but where a harder joint is required.

Tee Bridle

Mitered Corner Bridle Joints are used where a tougher joint than a mitered halving joint is required and where a molding, groove, or refund runs round the edge (e.g., mirror structures). Either or both sides of the outlet may be mitered as required.

Mitered Bridle   Dovetail Bridle

Dovetailed Bridle joints can be used where there is some propensity for the joint to be pulled apart.

14. Dowel Joint

Dowel joints are the most durable joint type when it comes to woodworking, especially when utilizing numerous rows of dowels. Dowels develop strong joints that are easy to create in your home. This joint is used for building reliable, accurate joints in timber.

Two Dowel Joint

They are thicker and more durable than nails or screws, and for that reason, they are much less susceptible to breaking.

They provide a stronger joint than just using adhesive.

This joint is pretty self-explanatory. As one of the many variations of a butt joint, the dowel joint is one of the most prominent joints.

It is used to make tabletops, cupboards, and chairs, to name a few. Dowel joints give the impression of a conventional butt joint.

The dowel joint uses round 'pins' (the dowels mentioned above) to hold the joint together.

These sorts of joints call for careful preparation and the adhesive to be as strong as possible.

You have to pierce two aligning holes that are half the depth of the dowel itself. You use adhesive in the holes to keep the dowel in nice and tight!

Dowels kept for use

Gradually the adhesive, naturally, can dry out.

Nonetheless, the advantage of a dowel joint is that typically the dowels will keep your piece together.

This creaking and contraction of the timber is one reason why dowel joints are not frequently used in higher-end hand-made furniture.

Box with Dowel Joint

Dowel Joint Pros

- Dowling is a quick process.
- It helps to ensure a smooth finish.
- Screws, nails, or other tools are not needed.
- Dowel joints are the strongest kinds of joints in woodworking, especially when using multiple rows of dowels.
- Dowels assist in producing solid joints that are easy to make in your home.

Dowel Joint Cons

- Misalignment of Joints
- Dowel Shearing
- No Face to Face Grain Union

15. Finger Joint

As per Wikipedia: *A finger joint is also called a comb joint; it is a woodworking joint made by cutting a collection of corresponding interlocking accounts in two kinds of wood, which are then glued. The cross-section of the joint resembles the interlocking of fingers between 2 hands; for this reason, the name "finger joint."*

A conical or scarfed finger joint is one of the most common joints used to create long lumber pieces from strong boards. The result is finger-jointed lumber. The finger joint can also be useful when creating walls, molding or trim, and can also be used in floorboards and door building.

Finger joints allow for more robust parts while considerably reducing waste (which saves money in the long run). The benefits of finger-jointed lumber are straightness and dimensional stability.

Finger Joints are used for various projects like:

- Board Door Frame
- Flooring
- Boxes

There are many variations of finger joints, such as :

Square finger joint

Stepped finger joint

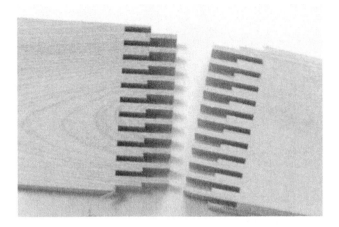

Slanted cut finger joint

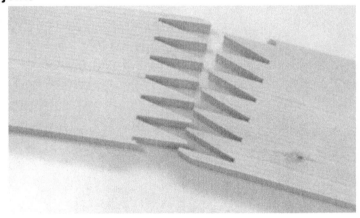

Finger Joint Pros

- Makes a straighter joint
- Much less timber is wasted
- Budget-friendly
- Resilient for an upright load
- Adhesives can be applied, allowing a more robust joint than mortise and tenon

Finger Joint Cons

- Can appear misaligned
- Harder to get a smooth wall

5. Japanese Joinery

Introduction

Unlike many traditional joinery techniques, Japanese joinery has until recently remained a closelipped craft among carpentry family members in Japan.

The detailed joints are made with precision and ability, making use of various end, corner, and intermediate joints to thoroughly counteract tons and torsions.

These have parts set up like puzzles to develop smart structures, which are understood to be among several of the oldest surviving structures today.

As opposed to the basic types of timber building, Japanese joinery doesn't depend on irreversible fixtures such as screws, nails, and adhesives. Instead, joints are securely safeguarded with interlocking connections.

Due to 3D visualizations, the intricacies behind these have been disclosed to crafters and manufacturers alike, offering the possibility to re-establish Japanese joinery into buildings.

Traditional Japanese Joinery

Centuries before the development of screws and fasteners, Japanese artisans used complex, interlacing joints to attach pieces of timber. I know it might be a bit more time consuming; however, I have started using Japanese joints to construct my recent furnishings. Using less hardware is a clear advantage.

Japanese carpenters can tell you a lot regarding a wood's quality and its suitability for a project.

Experienced woodworkers can differentiate between root and branch end, which helps in deciding where to divide the wood piece.

Also, they understand the type of timber through appearance, feel, and also odor, as well as how the timber was dried.

Many people don't demonstrate the skill they have. Japanese carpenters show their skill: the keshōmen, or "decorative face" of a piece of wood.

The distinct arch pattern you usually see on the face of a board is the result of "simple sawing." Ordinary sawing is one of the most efficient ways to cut a log, leaving the facility core to be used for columns. Yet, carpenters consider it to be the least sophisticated way for the timber.

The pattern is quite attractive, and plain-sawn lumber wastes extremely little wood, but the "arcs" that show up on the lumber's face also mean that it is somewhat weaker than a piece where the grain is vertical. Sometimes those arcs will split from the cut plane.

Additionally, an imperfect reducing blade may catch on the development rings and gash the wood.

Plain-sawn lumber tends to shrink more as it dries out, and may additionally "mug," its face becoming concave.

Due to this, Japanese woodworkers are specific concerning which side of a piece of lumber is the crucial face - the keshōmen to be displayed in the completed work - and which is inconsequential. When they make use of a plain-sawn board, the face displaying the grain's arches will always be dominant - but the unsightly end needs to be covered.

A great woodworker can tell whether the board is likely to cup, and will also ensure weak boards are not used where they will be seen.

Better Cuts for Stunning Grain

Quartersawn timber decreases the likelihood of issues of cupping, shrinkage, and splitting. However, this technique of cutting even more of the timber is a lot more work, making it extra pricey.

Nevertheless, every surface area of the board can conveniently be used as a keshōmen.

**Quartersawn lumber is the angle that the annular growth rings intersect the face of the board.

Types of Japanese Joints

- **Interlocking Tenon Joint:** Used for making a staircase or chair. Two or more pieces are attached.

- **Interlocking miter joint:** It's a half=lap type joint used in heavy frame construction.

- **Threeway corner miter joint:** Three pieces have miter here, with a leg feature as tenon, which fits with the other two pieces as shown below.

- **Three-way pinned corner miter joint:** This joint is similar to the earlier one but has an additional pin, as shown below.

- **Secret mitered dovetail joints**

  Also called full blind mitered joints, these joints are strong and suitable for cabinet and box works.

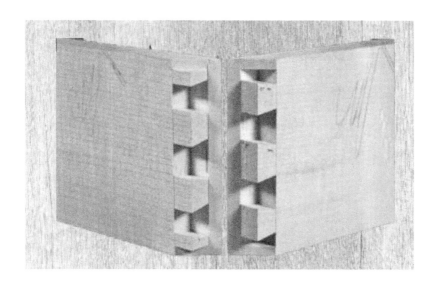

- **Shelf assistance joint:** This joint is used for cases where a heavy load is required to be held on the shelf. Dado shelf is used at the end of the shelf to support the load.

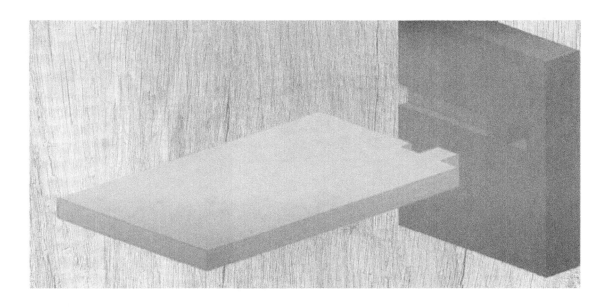

- **Divided mortise and tenon joint:**

Tenons cut into rails mesh together. These are used in large panels and frames.

- **Mitered shoulder tenon joint:** Similar to the last joint with one side of the mortise and tenon beveled as shown.

- **Sliding dovetail joint:** Used in chair construction to connect legs to the rail.

- **Mitered corner joint:** This joint is used predominantly in large structures/frames.

6. CNC Wood Joinery

Joinery is a part of woodworking that includes joining pieces of wood to create more complex products. Some timber joints utilize fasteners, bindings, or adhesives, while others use just wood aspects. The qualities of wooden joints like strength, adaptability, toughness, and appearance stem from the properties of the joining products and how they are used in the joints.

CNC Joints

CNC joinery differs from conventional woodworking joints. Round interior edges can create uncomfortable and even unpleasant joints. However, the ability to reproduce specific activities makes these joints a breeze.

Tolerance

The secret to good joinery is identifying the correct amount of tolerance.

"Tolerance describes the max error one can endure; according to the practical precision, one can anticipate from himself. Each people must establish his/her tolerance."

Considerations in CNC Cut Joinery

Below are the few factors to consider for CNC joinery.

Devices:

Instead of router bits, saw blades are used.

Wear and tear on the edge of the wood is much more problematic with router bits.

It requires meticulous setup, so the device works correctly.

Router bits exert more pressure on the workpiece while cutting and requiring stronger fixturing.

Routing plywood shape cuts are usually machined with a compression bit. This bit is lowered from the top as well as raised from the bottom to minimize tear in sheet woods.

Pockets are generally cut with down shear bits to reduce tear-out.

Corners:

Square corners can't be cut with cylindrical router bits. In several scenarios, this indicates joints need to be made with rounded corners.

The rounded corners can be pierced or routed.

A crucial point with routing these corners is that the tool must keep being moved while making the cut. Otherwise, extreme heat develops.

This will wear down the tool and create the risk of fire.

Tolerance:

Two mating parts won't fit together if cut the same size.

A void needs to exist between the parts for them to slide into one another as well as for adhesive.

In CNC, it's common to use a void of 0.005" per side of the joint. So, for instance, a tenon needs to be cut 2 times 0.005" narrower than the mortise (0.005" on each side). This is a rather limited fit yet will certainly work if the maker is accurate, and the tools are sharp.

If the devices are plain, then the cut will not be as tidy, and the precision can't be kept. Therefore, it is sometimes necessary to use 0.01" per side.

Wood:

Product thickness variants have a huge influence on the digital joints.

For a specific thickness, tool path programming will be done.

If the wood is not that specific density, it will affect the fit of the joint.

Because of this, "Wood to leave" and also "Flooring to leave" parameters in the CAM software program can offer offsets to make up for the variation.

Fixturing:

Rather than moving the job piece over the device, the job must be held firmly while the tool moves.

The procedure for safeguarding the work is called fixturing.

When it comes to 3-axis routing of plywood, this indicates tabbing the components. For hardwood, this typically involves double-sided tape holding the components to a spoil board.

CNC Cut Joint Examples:

There are several exciting joints that can be quickly cut on the CNC, which would be very time-consuming if made with standard shop tools.

Types of CNC joints:

3-Axis CNC Corner Joints

These joints affix members along an edge to create an edge, in 3-axis joinery, generally at 90 degrees.

- **Finger Tenons**

These are one of the simplest CNC joints which are exposed at the corner. Sufficient surface is available for glue.

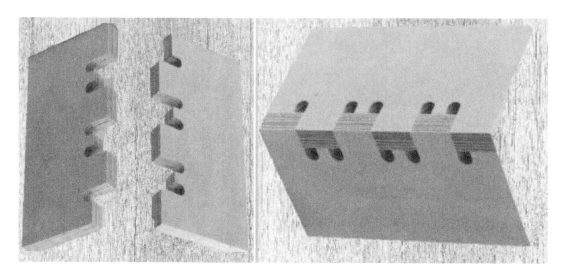

- **Blind Finger Tenons**

This uses pockets along the edge of the joint to stop the tenons from showing through. This is described as a blind joint. The sides are visible from the outside.

- **Lapped Fingertip Tenons**

This is a type of half-blind joint. It is made by cutting pockets for all the fingers to slot right into one side only.

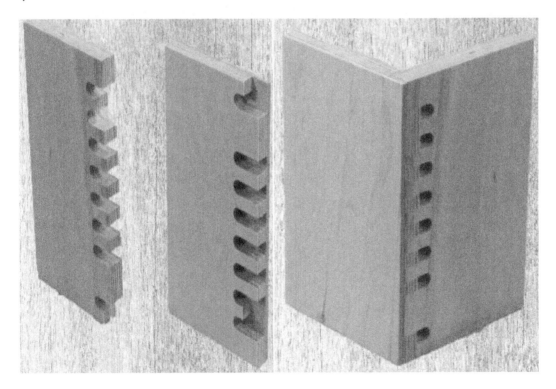

- **Fingertip Tenons**

The two parts are identical. They give a lot of adhesive areas and allow a stable connection. Here, the narrower tenons are referred to as "fingertip" as opposed to "finger."

71

- **Hammer Tenons**

This joint is made to keep the joint from pulling apart along one axis mechanically. You can see precisely how the fingers lock over the grooves in the mating fingers' edges. The name comes from the hammerhead form on the right. Some joints are created to break down or split conveniently.

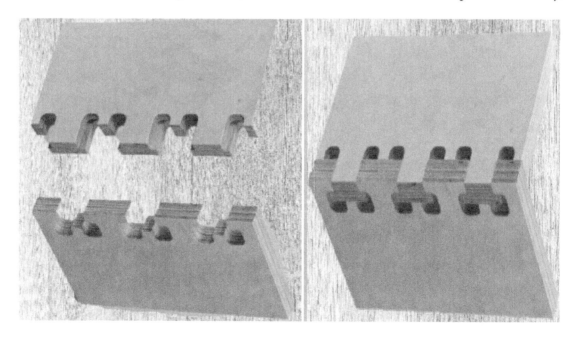

- **Fingertip Tenons along with key**

The lengthened tenons of this joint have a notch that accepts a key that protects the joint from tension.

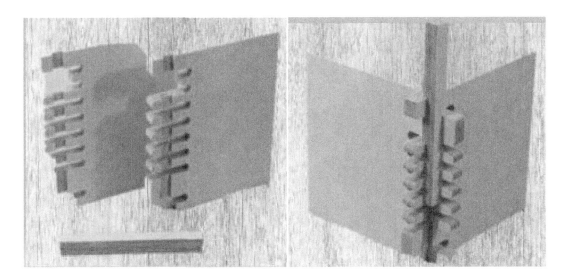

Right here, it partly removed, revealing the grooves in each wood.

- **Catch Tenon**

This is a type of break-down joint. The components are slid into each other, and the catch is pressed via the matching lock. The tenon flips down and hooks to protect the joint from splitting through stress.

The catch is pocked to the half-thickness to make it much easier to flex over the latch.

- **Doweled mortise and through tenon**

This example uses a dowel to prevent one part from sliding back through the other. When the dowel is tight versus the face of the mating wood, the joint is rather solid. Note that the joint above uses a drill to get rid of the edge product. Earlier joints used the router a bit. This decision has a significant effect on the look of the joint.

3-Axis CNC Housing Joints
These joints attach two parts in a perpendicular manner.

- ### Through Finger Tenons
This is an example of a through the joint where the tenons of the vertical participant show through the side.

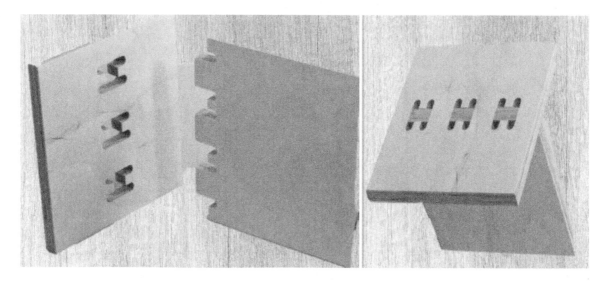

- ### Through Fingertip Tenons
This joint provides a greater surface area for the glue. Refer to the below picture:

- **Clip Tenons**

The long tenons flex just enough to allow them to get right into the mortises. When fully through, they hook over and below the mortises to lock them into place.

3-Axis CNC Structure Joints

These structure joints enable components to attach in a T or X arrangement. They are typically half-laps. That is, the product is removed from both pieces to permit them to overlap. Normally the product is removed midway through each piece.

- **Oval Shouldered Halving**

Basic curved edge half-lap joint. The components are identical. This joint is decoratively contrasted to a regular half-lap but is still steady. The curves give some extra tensile strength as well as a boosted glue area alongside the joint. In all half-lap joints, the product thickness is vital to a precise fit.

- **Dovetailed Cross Halving**

This joint has two of the same components. They provide a high level of racking resistance and a lot of glue area.

- **Jigsaw Cross Halving**

A joint is similar to the one over, although these parts are mirror images of one another.

- **Cross Miter Joint with Jigsaw Key**

This joint enables four different pieces to join up with an intersection area, making use of a jigsaw key. In a suitable tight joint, this is extremely challenging to take apart. In a joint loosened sufficiently where the joint can be easily uncoupled, the holding of the four members is not really inflexible.

The adhering of joints is done at a T junction instead of an X.

- **Stop Lap with Jigsaw Key**

This jigsaw essential offers some stress resistance. This joint additionally has a notch cut in the side so the cross participant can withstand lateral anxieties too.

- **Jigsaw Miter Joint**

An additional decorative half-lap corner joint that offers resistance to riving because of the interlocking components.

- **Miter Joint with Butterfly Key**

A butterfly key is used to hold the two pieces together. The thickness of the key is half the density of the material.

3-Axis CNC Edge-To-Edge Joints

These joints join two wood pieces end to finish or edge to edge.

Lapped Dovetail

This joint allows two boards to be connected along their edges. It has a beautiful decorative effect, and the dovetail form offers mechanical resistance against pulling apart. At the rear end of the joint, the edge is a straight line.

Dual Lapped Dovetail

Double dovetails are a variation. So the ornamental tails show up on each side of the wood.

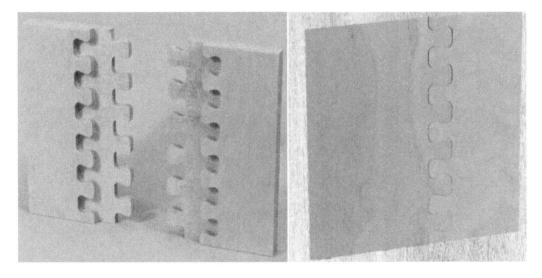

Board Extending with Jigsaw Keys

These joints use removable keys to join edges with the boards.

These keys are tough to get in as well as out of the pockets if the fit is excellent. So these are not suitable as knock-down (uncouple) joints.

Board Lengthening with Unbalanced Dovetail Keys

This is a joint that uses more commonly shaped dovetails. Butterfly keys resemble this although they are in proportion regarding their centerline (these are crooked).

Ginkgo Scarf with Stub Tenons

The form of this joint echoes the Ginko tree leaf and also demonstrates the convenience with which the CNC can cut complicated contours.

Gooseneck Mortise as well as Tenon Joint with Stub Tenons
Same principle as above – various types of geometry to this variation.

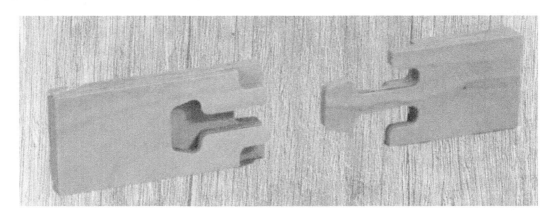

Dual Jigsaw
Both parts of this joint style are comparable but are mirror images of each other.

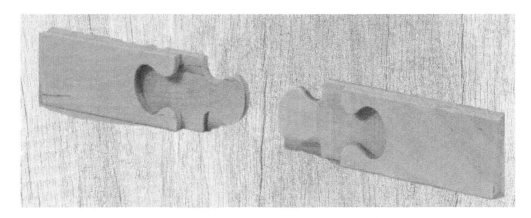

Halving with Elliptical Machine Tenon

This joint is used where the two parts are each thinned by one-half and overlap each other. The ellipse tenon in this joint provides mechanical resistance to pulling apart. This joint would be weak in wood because the sheer plane is alongside the wood fibers (so-called short-grain).

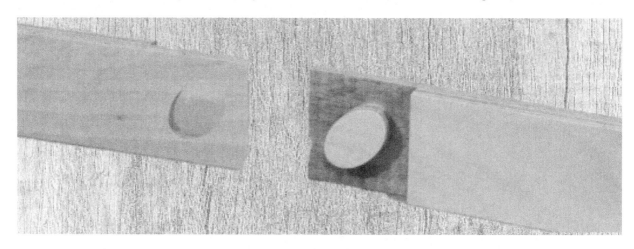

Triple Dovetail

Single dovetail on one side, double on the other. Unlike the joint over, these are not aligned side to side, making it stronger.

7. Joinery Projects for Beginners

1. Table Leg Assembly Using Mortise and Tenon Joinery

Materials:

- Wood board
- Wood glue
- Parallel clamps
- Spiral feather board
- Rubber mallet
- Table saw

One of the most basic joinery methods is mortise and tenon. This is a fantastic joint for table legs, and with a few tools, it can be very strong.

Milling and Marking

The first step is to get your wood and material for the project.

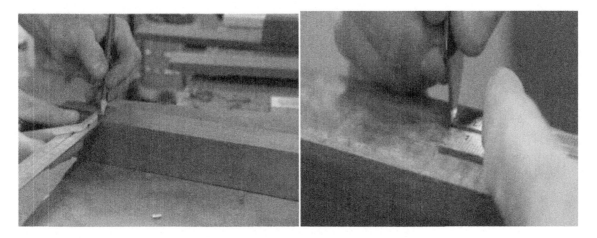

The more the wood is shaped and squared, the better for the project. If the timber is only recently dried, leave a day between each milling step.

This will allow the timber to move as the stress is released.

As soon as the wood is cut square and is sized, it's time to mark it out for the mortise, the holes in the legs.

In this situation, the rail will be the tenon, so all the rails must be of the same dimension.

A lot of hardwoods splinter quickly, so breaking the timber fibers along the line implies you'll have cleaner lines.

Use a combination square mark on the front-facing edge. Make this the same right around the table on each leg.

This line will be cut initially because it's what individuals will see, any modifications will be made on the line facing inwards.

The next step is to draw the line on the other side to represent the rail width. Then cut along the lines using a marking knife.

Eliminating Material from the Leg

After marking out the leg, we require the removal of the product.

Use a drill press to eliminate most of it. However, the router needs to be under as little stress as possible to guarantee a clean cut.

Drill a series of openings making use of a depth quit, leaving several millimeters before the line.

Now set up a stop block for the router, so you don't mistakenly cut too far, and begin getting rid of along the cut line.

Setup the fence on the router, so you're cutting on the line of the outdoor face of the rail/leg.

Do all the legs with this setting on the fencing, so they're the same.

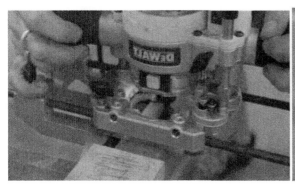

Beware cutting in both directions as the router will react in a different way to the feed direction.

This highlights the need to get rid of as much wood as possible using the drill press.

As soon as you've done all the legs with the fence one established, move to cut along the various other lines and repeat.

At this stage, the rails need to either be a tight fit or not be able to fit.

I prefer to cut the mortises undersize as well as sand the rails to fit. Cutting the mortise too large is not recommended.

Cut Rail

Cut the mortise into the leg to be smaller than the height of the rail.

Make a small notch out of the bottom of the rail in each edge, enough to ensure that the edge rests against the leg.

The sharper this cut is, the far better it will look. Use a marking knife to cut all the lines.

Glue

As you have a tight fit, you can glue the parts together.

Use clamps to draw the legs right into the rail.

You can improve with lots of practice and by not repeating mistakes.

2. Small Table with Pocket Hole Joinery

Materials:

- A pocket hole jig set
- Pocket screws drill and driver bar clamps
- (4) tapered legs 1 3/4" square by 10" tall (any size will do depending on your need)
- Some scrap birch or other wood for the stool skirt and saw of choice
- Stain and finish safety glasses

Getting the pieces all set

Initially tear up some scrap birch to 3" broad.

After that, cut two wood pieces 15 1/2" long for the sides as well as two pieces 8 1/4" for the ends.

Use the pocket opening jig to position screw holes on the top and end edges.

The screw holes will be within the constructed stool so they won't show.

Assembly

Make one side at a time.

Put glue on each end of an end piece.

Keep two legs upside down and clamp them to the center of the end piece.

The primary factor in using a clamp is that pocket screws will push away from the target timber sometimes and won't screw in straight.

After you insert the screws, you won't need the clamp any longer. Repeat the action on the opposite side.

Join both ends to both sides once more using a clamp.

Go easy with the adhesive. If adhesive spurts out, clean it up with a damp cloth quickly.

Adding a Top

Cut another piece of wood 11 1/2" by 19" to be the top.

It might fit as a top for your stool.

Run a grain of glue around the top of your stool. Center your stool and screw it to the top.

Sand the surface.

Stain and Finish

Use your selection of stain, preferably two layers.

For example, you can use excellent old Minwax tarnish, and leave it to completely dry.

The benefit of water-based finishes is that they dry out quickly. You can use three coats of water-based semi-gloss poly.

The stool was built-in around an hour approximately. Finishing would not take long. You have to wait a while between layers.

3. Box using Box Joint

Materials:

3-4" wide board

Scrap board

Router table and a 1/4" straight bit

Compound miter saw, or table saw

Planer/Joiner

Belt sander

Straight file

Some clamps

Prepare the sides

Plane your board to the preferred thickness. I used a 2.5" broad maple planed to 3/8" thickness.

Cut four sides. Tag each wood piece lightly with a pencil: front, back, left, and right—this aids in putting the tag at the top of each wood piece for positioning later.

Prepare the jig

For this box, I wanted 1/4" fingers. I placed a 1/4" straight bit into the router table and also set the height to be the thickness of my sides. A quick method to do this is to stack two wood pieces on top of each other with one offset from the other. Raise the router bit until it simply touches the offset wood on top. Do not change the height.

Take a piece of scrap wood and clamp it to your miter scale. In my situation, I required an added piece of scrap to provide an excellent securing surface on the back of the miter gauge. The front piece is flush with the surface of the router table; the 2nd clamping piece removes the router a little bit.

Turn on the router and rout a rectangle-shaped hole in the front piece of scrap. This hole will hold the jig "finger."

Cut a piece of wood, probably from your board, just a bit larger than your bit size, in my case 1/4" x 1/4" x ~ 2".

Fit the piece into the slot you cut in the jig board. File or sand it to a tight fit. Additionally, sand the bottom down.

Currently, realign the jig board on the router table, against the miter gauge. This time, however, you will secure the board offset from the bit by the width of the bit(1/4"). I used a 1/4" drill bit as a spacer in between the jig finger and the little router bit.

Clamp the jig board into place. Be sure you are gauging against the widest part of the router bit and that the fit is as specific as you can get. This action determines precisely how well the box will fit.

Cut the fingers on the first wood.

Now, you can start cutting the fingers. It is an excellent idea to do some test fingers on a couple of scrap wood pieces to evaluate the positioning of the jig. If the fingers don't fit very tightly, try the placement once again.

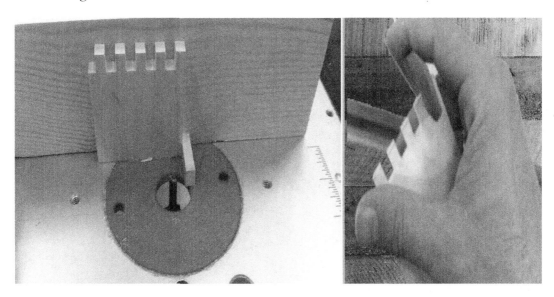

For the first cut: Straighten one side of the side wood with the inside side of the jig finger. Make a hole. You need a piece with a 1/4" square hole, 1/4" in from the left side.

For the second and following cuts: move the piece to ensure that the slot you cut fits over the jig finger. Create a brand-new hole. Repeat until you run out of the board. If the last hole doesn't straighten flawlessly with the side, do not worry, the corresponding piece will have the exact same quantity of leftover hole.

In between creating holes, mainly if the jig finger is a limited fit, you might want to run a square data with the newly reduced hole to change the fit. Don't file away too much, just enough for it to fit securely.

Cut the fingers on the second wood piece.
The second piece of wood is cut like the first one.

Evaluate your fit
Dry fit your wood. If it is too tight, attempt some light filing, if it is also loose, attempt once again with a much better dimension on the jig finger and the router bit placement.

Make the other two sides
Cut fingers on all eight sides, adhering to the same rules as the first two sides.

Bottom and Cover

For this box, I wanted a cover that would fit freely into the top and bottom. The miter gauge would help to keep the lid square when routing the short side.

Glue and finish

My box joint fingers were so tight that I had to use a club. The bottom wood glued in quickly, and the lid fits well at the top. Use stain or repaint as you want.

4. Chisel Box Using Japanese Joinery

Materials Required:

- Scrap Wood (If available, I recommend wood-paulownia wood)
- Chisel
- Hand Saw
- Planar
- Pencil

- Take out pieces of scrap wood and clean it of their coating and then shape them.
- The box has six sides, so pick two broader pieces for the base and lid and the leftover four for sides.
- Keep the largest chisel on the base and make lines for cutting in the shape of Japanese joinery, as shown below.

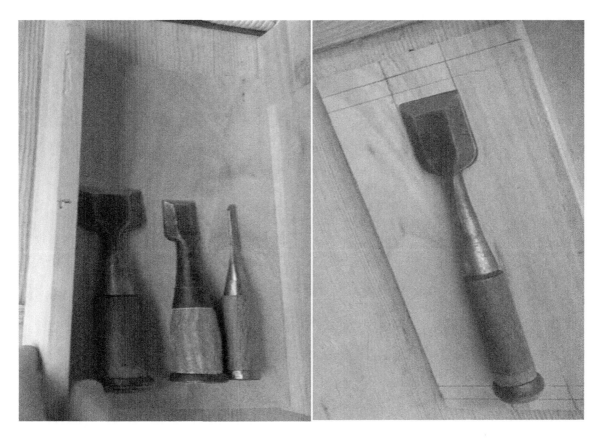

- Cut the mortise and tenon, as shown by the pencil in the base and side wood pieces.
- Measure the side joint as per the tenon in the base joint, as shown below. Carve out the tenon in the side wood piece as per this measurement.

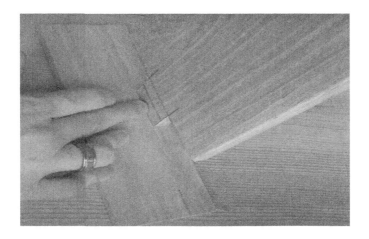

- Carve out similar tenon and mortise respectively on the other end of the wood pieces.
- Make similar length and breadth pieces of the box with similar mortise and tenon measurements.
- Run a dry fit, as shown in the below picture. (Without lid)

- Carve out the lid as per the measurement of the base wood piece.
- Cover the box with the lid.
- Go ahead with the finishing and coloring as per your choice.

5. Bench

Material Required

- Wood Piece (You need 2 leg,1 leg joiner, and 1 lid piece)
- Smoothing Plane
- Table Saw
- Marking Gauge
- Hand Saw
- Driller
- Chisel
- Marking Knife
- Sander

- Break down the wood and do the milling process to make the wood flat, square, and smooth.
- Alternatively you can buy S4S lumber (already milled on four sides).

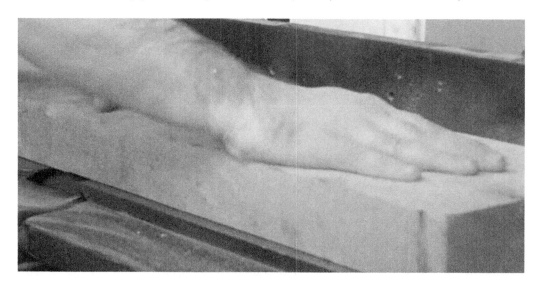

- Apply glue to the two boards, as shown below.
- Use the clamp and apply pressure to stick them.

- After the glue has dried, pass the joined plank through the thickness planar. Then apply a smoothing plane to all the wood pieces.

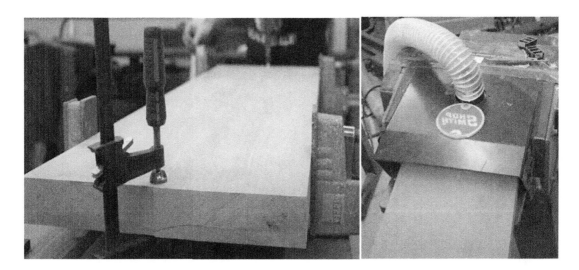

- The first joinery would be tenon on the end of the stretcher that will span between the legs.
- Use a measuring gauge to mark the tenon size and cut using a hand saw. Remove the material from the edges as marked to create a shoulder.
- After making the wedge cut, the slots are where the wedges would go inside.

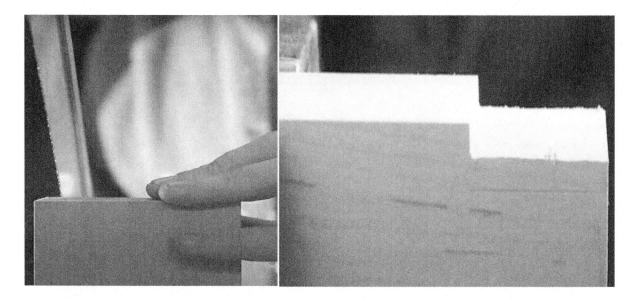

- There are many ways to make a hole. You can use driller first and chisel later to create the desired hole/mortise, as shown below. Repeat the process and make mortise and tenon on all the pieces.

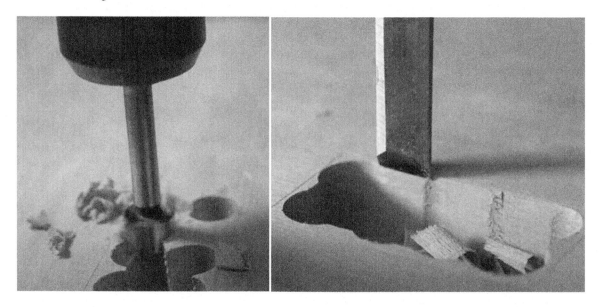

- The legs will be connected by one wood piece through a single joint and with the top lid through a double joint, as shown below.

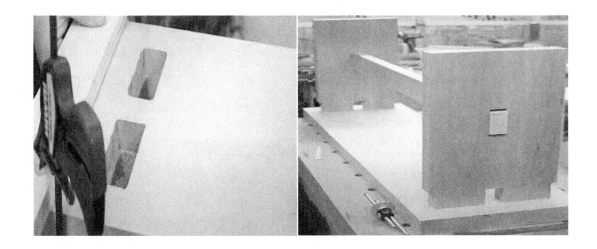

- Make the lid as with two holes on each side and measurement as per the tenon made before.

- Put glue into all the joints after getting tenons into the mortise.
- Sand the surface.
- Apply stain/paint of your choice for finishing.

- After applying 2-3 coats of finishing, below is the final bench.

8. Glossary

Box -A corner joint with interlacing square fingers. It receives pressure from two directions.

Bridle - The bridle joint is commonly defined as the opposite of a mortise and tenon, and is also mainly used in the woodworking and even joinery professions.

The name most likely came about because it bears some similarity to the fashion in which a bit goes into an equine's mouth and is also fastened to the bridle.

Butt - Completion of a piece of timber is stuck versus one more piece of wood. This is the simplest, as well as the weakest joint. Below are the types of butt joint:
a) T-butt b) end-to-end butt c) miter butt and d) edge-to-edge butt.

Glued - The glued joint is made by planing two pieces of hardwood to ensure that when positioned together, they are in contact with each other at every point. They are then typically joined with glue. These are known as a butt joint, snag joint, the slipped joint, or slapped joint.

Halved - The halved joint is often referred to as half-lapping. It is formed after halving the two pieces, i.e., by cutting half the depth of the wood away. There are, however, exceptions to this regulation, as in the case of "three-piece halving" (or, as it is in some cases called "third lapping") and in the halving of lumber with rebated or built edges. Halving is just one of the easiest methods of linking two wood pieces, precisely where it is desired to make frames.

Lap - Completion of a piece of timber is laid over and linked to another piece of wood. Because of a large area of long-grain to long-grain timber as well as adhesive surface insurance coverage, this is a very solid joint.

Mitering - The term mitering is normally used to signify the kind of joint used at the corner of an image frame; or where two pieces of timber are beveled away so as to fit each other, as the skirting or plinth mold. In these cases, the hardwood is cut to ensure that the joint goes to 45 degrees to the face, and also, the two pieces, when put together, develop an angle of 90 levels (a right angle).

Mortise and Tenon - A mortise and a tenon joint is a kind of joint that links two pieces of wood or other material. Woodworkers all over the world have used it for hundreds of years to join timber, mainly when the adjoining wood pieces attach at an angle of 90 °. In its basic form, it is both simple and solid.

Saddle - The "saddle joint" is used for connecting upright messages to heads of the framework, and definitely takes its name from its resemblance to how the saddle fits the steed. It does not damage the framework as a mortise and tenon joint does, and shrinkage has little impact upon the joint.

Headscarf - The approach known as "scarfing" is used for the joining of lumber towards its size, making it possible for the worker to create a joint with a smooth or flush look on all its faces. One of the simplest forms of the scarfed joint is known as a half lap.

Tongued as well as Grooved - The tongued and grooved joint is used throughout the entirety of the woodworking trades, as it does, a great range of work from the laying of flooring boards to the construction of cabinets, bookcases and also various other cabinet work. As the name of the joint indicates, on one board, a groove is created, on the joining board, a tongue is produced, and the two are matched with each other.

Batten
A slim strip of timber.

Beaded timber.
A basic round molding. Likewise, see molded wood.

Bevel
An angle, however, not an ideal angle. A sloping or canted surface area.

Casing
The lumber cellular lining of a door opening.

Cellular wood panel
Comparable to blackboard and batten board panels but the battens and laths create the core and are spaced either parallel or in lattice type. Panels are relatively light yet have some strength.

Chamfered
The sides have been removed lengthwise at an angle.

Cup
To bend as a result of shrinkage, particularly across the width of a piece of timber.

Dado
The lower part of an indoor wall, usually specified with a molded rail.

Thickness
The mass of a substance, generally shown in kg/cubic meters.

Distortion
Change in wood or timber-based material caused by shrinkage as the timber dries out. This includes bowing, twisting, and cupping.

Dovetail
One-piece has a splayed shape - like a dove's tail - and fits into the second piece's socket or eye.

Doweling
Round piece or length of timber. Also known as finished wood.

Drip groove
A groove cut or molded in the underside of a door or window sill to stop rain running back to the wall.

Dry board
See Damp handling.

Edge and end spacing
Spacing's in between bolts and the sides as well as ends of the parts that are being joined.

End grain
The revealed face of hardwood created when it's punctured a plane that's vertical to the grain.

End-jointed
See Finger-jointed.

Finger-jointed
Also called end-jointed. Much shorter pieces of wood are joined to create a much longer piece. The joint resembles interlaced fingers.

Grain
The basic direction of timber fibers or the pattern generated on the surface of lumber by cutting through the fibers. Also, see End grain and Brief grain.

Groove
A long slim channel. Likewise, see Tongued as well as grooved.

Kerf
The groove cut by a saw.

Knot
The remains of a branch in wood. A branch sawn off near the trunk naturally creates noise or a live knot. A busted branch stub that comes to be surrounded by brand-new growth produces a loosened or dead knot in the hardwood.

Mitre
Two pieces of wood form an angle or joint created between two pieces of timber by cutting bevels at equal angles in the ends of each wood.

Rotating cut

The log is installed in a large lathe and turned against the blade, which peels off the veneers in long sheets. Additionally called peeling or cutting.

Tenon

The end of the wood that's been lowered in section to suit a recess or cavity of the exact same size or a forecasting tongue on the end of a piece of wood which matches an equivalent mortise.

Tongue

A decrease in the thickness of the edge of a board. Also, see Tongued and also grooved.

V- jointed

Generally, tongued and grooved wood with a V-shaped channel in the facility of the board.

Veneer

A slim or fine sheet of timber created by rotary-cutting, peeling or cutting.

Woodblock

Timber block is a floor covering made from little strips or blocks of timber, around three inches wide and nine inches long, prepared in herringbone, basket-weave, and various other geometric patterns.

Timber planks

Planks in long sizes with sizes of four inches or more.

Timber strip

Narrower and shorter boards than planks and have up to three strips of wood per board.

9. Conclusion

So this brings us to the end of our current discussion on wood joinery. We have discussed traditional joinery, Japanese joinery, and CNC joinery. No matter which form you use, the concept remains the same.

Finally a few tips for beginners:

- Avoid working with freshly cut lumber, as this will shrink after the joint is assembled. Use wood that has dried and is ready for the outside environment in which the finished product will be used.

- When making a furniture piece that will need to bear a heavy load, use bigger joints or joints with bigger architectural natures, such as twin mortise-and tenons. This will certainly distribute the load over a broader location and reduce stress on the joint. If the layout of a piece limits using big joints, utilize a number of smaller sized joints to spread out the weight as well as lower stress

- Make sure the parts of a joint are effectively proportioned. If a tenon in a mortise-and-tenon joint is too thick, the mortise participant will be weakened

- When setting up the mating boards of a joint, think about the grain direction of the elements, and oriented woods to make up for the wood activity.

- Cut the components of a joint parallel to the grain.

- For some joints, such as dovetails, utilize the completed part of the joint (the pins) to format the mating part to make it accurate.

- Make use of the proper measuring and marking devices for making joints.

- If a joint requires support, use glue along with fasteners, dowels, biscuits, or splines.

This brings the end of our discussion. I hope you liked the content. I would appreciate it if you could share your feedback and reviews on the platform. You can also reach me at valueadd2life@gmail.com.

Practice safely!

Stephen

My Other Books in DIY series:

Printed in Great Britain
by Amazon